THE GREAT MONKEY TRIAL

TOM McGOWEN

THE GREAT MONKEY TRIAL

SCIENCE VERSUS
FUNDAMENTALISM
IN AMERICA

FOREWORD BY
STEPHEN JAY GOULD

Barbara Silberdick Feinberg, Consulting Editor

FRANKLIN WATTS
A TWENTIETH CENTURY
AMERICAN HISTORY BOOK
NEW YORK LONDON TORONTO
SYDNEY 1990

Library of Congress Cataloging-in-Publication Data

McGowen, Tom.

The great monkey trial : science versus fundamentalism in
America / by Tom McGowen.

p. cm.—(A Twentieth century American history book)
Includes bibliographical references.

Summary: Examines the Scopes trial concerning the teaching of
evolution in public schools, its outcome, and the implications for
the continuing debate between evolutionists and creationists.

ISBN 0-531-10965-8

1. Scopes, John Thomas—Trials, litigation, etc.—Juvenile
literature.   2. Evolution—Study and teaching—Law and legislation
—Tennessee—Juvenile literature.   [1. Scopes, John Thomas—Trials,
litigation, etc.   2. Evolution—Study and teaching—Law and
legislation.]   I. Title.   II. Series.

KF224.S3M35   1990
344.73'077—dc20
[347.30477]   90-33610   CIP   AC

*To Ron, Dave, Bleue, Penny, Joy, Toni,
Linda, and all the rest of the helpful staff
of the Eisenhower Library*

CONTENTS

THE GREAT MONKEY TRIAL

FOREWORD

Two exciting events of my childhood inspired me to become a paleontologist (a scientist who studies the history of life on earth as revealed in the evidence of fossils):¹ my first view of dinosaur skeletons at the American Museum of Natural History in New York at age five, and my discovery, through reading several books as a young teenager, that evolution provided the central theme for understanding and interpreting the history of life.

Evolution is one of the half dozen or so grandest and most exciting concepts that science has ever developed. Evolution is powerfully supported by a vast range of facts from all areas of biological research: paleontology, genetics, embryology, geographic distribution, classification of organisms, anatomy, etc. Scientists are therefore as confident of its basic truth as about anything else that we have ever discovered. It is no exaggeration to say that we are as sure evolution occurred as we are that the earth revolves around the sun, and not the sun around the earth. (We remain, however, quite uncertain about many aspects of how evolution works, and scientists are now engaged in fruitful debates about mechanisms of evolutionary change. Science is most interesting when it engages in such useful debates.) Evolution intrigues and excites us because its scope is so broad and its subject matter includes so many deep questions of fundamental interest to all thinking people: What are our relationships with other living things? When did life start? How did it change through time? When did humans arise?

Yet while evolution has excited so many people, it has also disturbed others. Science has the general property of debunking hopeful myths that we construct about the natural world in order to increase our unjustified sense of cosmic importance. The myth that the earth is just a few thousand years old, that humans have been part of this history for all but the first few days of creation, and that humans have the right to rule both the planet and all other animals by virtue of superior intelligence is a story that gives comfort to many people. But it is false, and false myths can only harm us in the long run. Among the finest sayings of Jesus, we read: "Ye shall know the truth, and the truth shall make you free" (John 8:32).

There is no real conflict between science and religion because the two fields are so different in their aims and methods. Science tries to understand and interpret the factual state of the world; religion deals with ethics and values. The great majority of scientists and theologians in modern America accept this interpretation and see no conflict whatever between an acceptance of evolution and the practice of religion. But an important social and political movement in America, which is called fundamentalism and quite strong in some regions of the country (though weak to nearly nonexistent in others), insists that the Bible be read as literally and factually true in every word. Fundamentalists have attacked evolution because scientific fact does conflict with the literal claim that the earth is just a few thousand years old, that organisms were all created in six days, and that a great flood recently covered the earth, destroying all nonmarine life not saved on Noah's ark. As I wrote above, this debate is not a conflict between science and religion (since the great majority of religious leaders in America have no quarrel with evolution and do not view evolution as a threat to their subject), but between science and systems of belief that may bring comfort to many people, but are false.

In any case, fundamentalists have been trying to weaken, or even to ban, the teaching of evolution in public schools ever since the 1920s. The most famous episode in this history, the Scopes Trial of 1925, is the subject of this excellent book. But the story has continued. In the early 1980s two states, Arkansas and Louisiana, passed laws requiring that creationism be given "equal time" if evolution were taught in science classes of public schools. Both these laws were tested in federal courts and declared contrary to the First Amendment of the United States Constitution (the freedom-of-religion guarantee), and therefore invalid. In 1987, the United States Supreme Court upheld these decisions, thus ending a drama that began more than 60 years ago in Dayton, Tennessee.

I was one of six expert witnesses (including scientists and theologians) at the first of these trials in Arkansas in late 1980. Clarence Darrow brought expert witnesses to Dayton in 1925, but as this book discusses, they were not allowed to testify. Thus, our testimony represented the first and only time that our side was able to present its full intellectual case in a courtroom. (The Louisiana law was declared invalid without trial on the basis of the Arkansas decision.) On the witness stand, I remember feeling a surge of excitement as I thought about John Scopes and sensed my great privilege in being a tiny part of a drama that forms a major episode of American social history in the twentieth century.

—Stephen Jay Gould

1

THE HISTORICAL
BACKGROUND OF
THE SCOPES TRIAL

In a small town in Tennessee in the year 1925, there took place one of the most controversial and widely watched trials to be held in the United States during the twentieth century. It was not a trial for murder, robbery, treason, nor any other such popularly newsworthy event; it was actually of far more significance than any such thing as that. From one viewpoint, it was a trial to determine whether the schools of the United States would be free to teach what was regarded as unquestionable scientific fact or would be prevented from such teaching because it conflicted with the religious beliefs of a certain group of citizens. From another viewpoint, it was a trial to prevent the teaching of a false, wicked idea that tore young people away from the faith and morality in which they had been reared. Basically, it was a confrontation that pitted modern scientific knowledge against the Old Testament stories of the Bible.

The roots of this confrontation actually extended far back into the past. For about the first 1,400 years of the Christian religion, no Christian wondered much about such things as the origin of the world, the beginning of life, or the earth's place in the universe. The answers to those questions and all others were in the Bible, and almost everyone simply accepted them. But with the beginning of what we now call science, some five hundred years ago, problems arose. Some of the first scientists began trying to find real answers to things, instead of simply accepting what religion taught or what had always just been *believed*, and their answers sometimes conflicted with what the Bible said. In 1543, a Polish astronomer known as Nicolaus Copernicus published a book in which he offered physical and mathematical proofs to show that the earth moved around the sun. Until then, almost everyone had believed that the earth was the center of the universe and the sun went around *it*, so Copernicus's discovery was astonishing and rather humbling for most people—if the earth was just another planet, whirling around the sun like the other plain planets, then neither it nor the people on it seemed quite as important. And it quickly dawned on some people that Copernicus's discovery and what it meant did not quite agree with what the Bible seemed to say. Religious leaders soon decided that Copernicus's newly discovered knowledge was dangerous to religion, and they tried to prevent it from spreading, even going so far as to execute several men and to imprison the famous scientist Galileo for believing in Copernicus's findings and teaching them. But the truth of Copernicus's discovery was obvious; more and more evidence came to light to support it, and in time it became recognized as an established fact by everyone except a very few churchmen who simply insisted that, despite any evidence to the contrary, the Bible *had* to be right.

Over the next four centuries numerous scientific discoveries were made in every field, and many of these began to add up to create a rift between scientific fact and religious belief. The discovery of fossil plants and animals showed that many kinds of extremely different unknown creatures had lived on the earth in the past. The discovery that the rock forming the earth's surface is in layers, with the oldest rock at the bottom and the newest at the top, and the discovery that each layer contains specialized kinds of fossils that are mostly different from those in other layers indicated that living things had steadily changed over the ages. The discovery that rock is not an ageless, unchanging material but is formed within the earth by heat, or on sea bottoms by *sedimentation* (the slow buildup of sand and other substances), and pushed up to the surface by earthquakes and volcanic activity and then worn down by erosion, showed that the earth itself had changed over the ages. That confirmed that the world was far, far older than the six-thousand-some years religious leaders claimed it to be, based on the Bible.

But the scientific idea that broke the rift wide open was that of the English naturalist (a scientist who studies plants and animals in their natural environments) Charles Darwin. This was the idea of the process known as evolution (meaning "gradual development"), the process by which all living things are slowly and continuously changed over many millions of years, causing new species to emerge and old ones to die out.

Darwin was not actually the first person to come up with the idea of evolution; a number of others had considered it. More than 2,500 years ago, ancient Greek scholars had speculated that certain kinds of sea animals had changed into land animals by having parts of their bodies adapt to life on land. A Greek named Empedocles suggested that animals that adapted became better able to survive, whereas creatures that could not adapt eventually died out. In 1682 an early English scientist, John Ray, stated that all forms of life were linked together in a kind of chain, with each "link" having something in common with the one before it. In the 1700s a French nobleman,

★ 19 ★

the Comte de Buffon, came to the conclusion that there were tiny, barely noticeable differences between generations of species of creatures, and that in time, these differences produced new kinds of creatures. Another French noble, the Chevalier de Lamarck, suggested that changes in the environment could cause animals to adapt until, after many generations, new forms of animals appeared that were better suited to the changed environment. However, all these ideas were largely just speculation, built on sound reasoning, but without any real evidence to back them up. It was Darwin who put in the long years of study and experimentation, linking together the work of other scientists to produce the first evidence for evolution and a theory, or explanation, for why evolution takes place.

In general, Darwin's theory pointed out that most living things produce far more offspring than the environment could possibly support (for example, a single female frog may lay several thousand eggs at a time) but that most of these offspring will not survive; they are kept in check by lack of food, being preyed on by other creatures, and being killed off by environmental changes. However, no two members of any species of plant or animal are exactly alike—they all have different combinations of traits—and Darwin believed that some members of every generation of a species have special traits that help them to survive. Thus, they are more likely to live longer and produce offspring that will inherit their traits, making it easier for the offspring to survive and continue to pass along the helpful traits to their young, whereas members of the species without such traits tend to eventually get weeded out. Darwin called this "survival of the fittest," meaning that those creatures best able to survive will survive. He felt that over a long period of time—many millions of years— this natural weeding-out process, or "natural selection" of those creatures best able to survive longer, produced new species of creatures and the old species became extinct. He suggested that all life had begun from a *first* single-cell organism that had evolved into a more complicated form and that evolution had continued, creating many different forms of organisms. Thus, of course, Darwin's theory meant that every species of present-day plant and animal is descended from some earlier, similar form of life, and it indicated that humans, as well as present-day apes, were descended from a common apelike ancestor of millions of years ago.

Darwin first presented his theory at a meeting of scientists in 1858 and published it a year later in a book called *On the Origin of Species by Means of Natural Selection, or the Preservation of Favoured Races in the Struggle for Life.* Like most new scientific ideas and theories, these ideas of Darwin's set off a great deal of argument and controversy. However, whereas most such controversy is usually just between scientists who agree or disagree with an idea, the controversy over Darwin's theory also involved religious leaders. The whole idea of evolution was in direct contradiction to the Bible, which states that all animal and plant species were created at the same time, exactly as they are now, and that all humans are descended from an original man and woman, Adam and Eve.

Debate began to rage throughout Darwin's homeland, England, with a few scientists taking Darwin's side immediately and most others, including many religious leaders, ranged against his theory. But it is a common happening in science that any theory based on incorrectly understood evidence or faulty reasoning eventually gets demolished by the work of other scientists, whereas a theory based fully on fact gains strength as new evidence comes to light, as was the case with Copernicus's theory that the earth revolved around the sun. And even as the arguments about evolution were going on, new evidence was accumulating to back up Darwin's theory. The discovery of gorillas by the Western world, during the mid-1800s, showed that there could be such a thing as a large, humanlike ape, which some scientists had doubted. The discovery in 1856 of fossil skeletons of an apparently different human species (the people we now call Neanderthals) showed that there had indeed been a more primitive kind of human. And the discovery of the fossil remains of a prehistoric creature that was clearly a combination of both reptile and bird (now called Archaeopteryx*) was a titanic piece of proof for Darwin's claim that birds had evolved from reptiles. It wasn't long before a majority of British scientists began to agree that Darwin was right. The evidence he presented, the reasoning of his theory, and the new evidence that was accumulating were all simply overwhelming.

And more and more evidence continued to accumulate. In America, paleontologists were finding thousands of fine fossils of prehistoric reptiles and mammals, and eventually there were enough available so that by viewing the skeletons of an animal such as the horse, from many different periods of time, a clear pattern of its evolution could actually be seen. The work of the Austrian monk-botanist Gregor Mendel, in crossbreeding pea plants by the thousands and studying the development of traits in each generation, proved Darwin's idea that traits were handed down and strengthened from generation to generation. Thus, by the beginning of the twentieth century, virtually all scientists working in the fields of biology, zoology, botany, geology, and paleontology (the study of ancient life forms), throughout the world, had accepted evolution as an absolute fact. There was still some uncer-

---

* In 1987, a charge was made that the Archaeopteryx fossil was a fake. A careful examination by a team of scientists from several different fields, using the most modern techniques available, proved that it was not.

tainty and argument over parts of Darwin's *theory*—whether it fully explained how and why evolution operated—but there was no doubt at all about the existence of the process of evolution.

In addition to all of this scientific work on evolution, scholars of the 1800s had also done a great amount of study of the Bible, reading it in its oldest forms in the ancient Greek and Aramaic languages. They found that the Old Testament had been written over a period of many hundreds of years by many different persons, and much of it had apparently been "borrowed" from primitive myths and legends of ancient Sumer and other very early nations of the Near East. This added to the realization that portions of the Bible were simply fable and that scientific discoveries throwing doubt on them were accurate.

As a result of all this, many Christian religious leaders throughout the world fully accepted the fact of evolution, the evidence for the vast age of the earth, and other recent scientific discoveries. Instead of viewing such findings as a threat to religion, they viewed them as evidence of the tremendous intellect of the Creator. In 1886, one of the foremost Protestant religious leaders of the United States, the Reverend Henry Ward Beecher, publicly stated that he believed evolution to be ". . . the discovery of the Divine method in creation," and proclaimed that the knowledge of evolution, rather than causing trouble for religion, would strengthen it. By 1900 Christian leaders of many mainline Protestant churches had adjusted the teachings of their churches to the facts of modern science, no longer requiring their church members to believe such biblical statements as that the earth had been created in six days, that the plants and animals had all been created exactly as they now are, and that the human race had been started by Adam and Eve.

However, there were many Christians, especially in

the United States, who absolutely refused to accept such changes. For them, the Bible simply could not be wrong, and they denied the accuracy of any evidence that indicated it was. Early in the twentieth century a number of small pamphlets entitled *The Fundamentals* were published and widely circulated throughout the nation. These pamphlets presented arguments intended to show that all of the statements in the Bible *had* to be true and could not be questioned, or else the Christian religion would be meaningless. Millions of American Christians accepted these arguments and began a movement that became known as Fundamentalism, a movement based on absolute, unyielding belief in everything that was said in the Bible. Many of these people broke away from churches that had become "modernized" by accepting evolution, and they started new churches founded on the old pre-evolution beliefs. In some cases, Fundamentalists were able to influence, to a large extent, several major churches such as the Baptist and Presbyterian denominations. By the 1920s, Fundamentalism was a major force in American religion.

By that time, evolution was being taught regularly as the basis of biology in almost every college and high school in the nation. The biology textbooks in use presented evolution as an established fact and discussed Darwin's discovery as one of the major scientific achievements of history. To Fundamentalists, this was horrifying. It represented an attack on their basic beliefs and a threat to the righteous upbringing of their children. They further felt that the teaching of evolution caused trouble for the nation and the world. A prominent Fundamentalist wrote: "All the ills from which America suffers can be traced back to the teaching of evolution!"

Leading Fundamentalists determined to launch an attack against the teaching of evolution in an effort to protect their children and, in their opinion, to save the entire nation from falling prey to atheism (disbelief in God) and the breakdown of morality that they felt belief in evolution caused. It was this attack that led directly to the trial in Tennessee in 1925.

2

SETTING THE STAGE
FOR THE TRIAL

The Fundamentalists had their work cut out for them. They concentrated on trying to get laws against the teaching of evolution passed first in various states where there were large numbers of Fundamentalists living, who would favor such a law.

In order to get a law passed by a state legislature, a member of the legislature must present a "bill" (a written document), which states the subject of the proposed law. The bill must be approved by a committee that deals with matters of the sort covered in the bill, and must then be voted on by both of the two "houses" of the legislature. If it gets a favorable vote in both houses it is sent to the governor of the state. If he signs the bill, it becomes a state law. So prominent Fundamentalists talked to Fundamentalist politicians who were members of state legislatures, urging them to produce anti-evolution bills. Non-Fundamentalist politicians were subjected to arguments, wheedling, promises, and various pressures to support such bills. Fundamentalist newspaper publishers and editors crusaded for anti-evolution laws, trying to mold public opinion so that politicians would take notice.

In 1922 a bill to forbid the teaching of "Darwinism, atheism, agnosticism [the belief that it isn't possible to know if there is or isn't a God] or the theory of evolution insofar as it pertains to the origin of man," reached a final vote in the state legislature of Kentucky. It was barely defeated, 42 votes to 41. Interestingly enough, the man who cast the decisive vote against the bill was actually a Fundamentalist, who voted against the bill because he felt that such a law would be "an infringement of personal liberty."

Also in 1922, in South Carolina, a bill to withhold money from any school that taught "the cult known as Darwinism," was defeated. In 1923 a bill similar to the one introduced in Kentucky was beaten in Florida, although the legislature passed a resolution (a suggestion, not a law) urging teachers not to teach "Darwinism or any other hypothesis that links man in a blood relationship to any other form of life." An anti-evolution bill was introduced into the Georgia legislature but was never sent to either of the two houses for a vote. A bill that won by a 71–34 vote in the lower house of the Texas legislature was allowed to simply "die" by not being sent to the upper house for a vote. A modest victory was gained in Oklahoma, when a bill prohibiting statements about evolution from appearing in textbooks was passed, but this did not actually halt the teaching of evolution. In 1924 an anti-evolution bill introduced into the legislature of North Carolina was defeated, but all biology textbooks covering evolution were removed from use in the state's high schools.

Despite all such disappointments and minor victories, the Fundamentalists continued their efforts. And in 1925 they scored their first resounding victory. In Tennessee a bill known as the Butler Act was passed, and it became against the law to teach evolution in any of Tennessee's public schools.

The Butler Act was the work of a man named John Washington Butler, a prosperous farmer who lived in the northern part of Tennessee. He was apparently a very decent, well-liked man, and in 1922 a number of his neighbors had persuaded him to run for the state legislature. Like just about everyone else in his area, he had been reared with a firm belief in the absolute truth of everything in the Bible, and when he started campaigning for office he made it plain that he opposed the teaching of evolution. However, he was actually less opposed to it on religious grounds than he was on the grounds of what he considered a lack of fairness—he felt it was unfair for the state schools, which were supported by the taxes of people like himself, mostly Fundamentalists, to teach something that might undermine the religious beliefs of the children of the people who paid those taxes. He was overwhelmingly elected to the state legislature in 1922 and reelected in 1924. That year, on his forty-ninth birthday, he wrote out the anti-evolution law that had been on his mind for some time, and later presented it to the legislature.

The Butler Act began with a preamble that described itself as "AN ACT prohibiting the teaching of evolution theory" and continued: "BE IT ENACTED BY THE GENERAL ASSEMBLY OF THE STATE OF TENNESSEE, That it shall be unlawful for any teacher in any of the universities, Normals [schools where high school graduates were trained as teachers], and all other public schools of the State which are supported in whole or in part by the public school funds of the State, to teach any theory that denies the story of the Divine Creation of man as taught in the Bible, and to teach instead that man has descended from a lower order of animals." Another section stated that any teacher found guilty of violating the act would be fined not less than $100 nor more than $500, which were fairly large sums of money at that time, when the average pay of a Tennessee teacher was $634 a year.

The bill was introduced into the lower house of the legislature and brought to a vote. Many members who voted for it were Fundamentalists who were, of course, sincerely in favor of it, but other members later admitted they had voted for the bill merely because they didn't want to be "shown up" as being against it and felt sure it would be defeated in the upper house anyway. But exactly the same thing happened in the upper house, with many legislators voting for the bill even though they were against it, because they didn't want to disclose their real position and felt sure the governor would prevent it from passing into law even if it won the vote. However, the governor, finding himself "on the spot," signed the bill into law, assuring himself, as he later stated in a message to the legislature, that he didn't think the law would ever be enforced anyway. Thus, apparently because a number of legislators were unwilling to vote according to their true beliefs, Tennessee became the first state to have an anti-evolution law, on March 21, 1925.

In the United States, the Constitution—the set of rules and principles that defines the powers of the government and the rights of the people—has force over all national and state laws. Technically, no law can ever stay in effect, anywhere in the nation, that contradicts the statements that are written in the Constitution. For example, no state could ever pass a law declaring that only one religion must be followed in the state, because the Constitution says, in effect, that every American is free to follow the religion of his or her choice (or to follow no religion at all, if they wish), and thus there can be as many different religions as people might want. A law attempting to allow only one religion would contradict that and would be called "unconstitutional." Each state also has its own constitution, based strongly on the national one, and no state can have laws that contradict its own constitution.

However, sometimes a law gets passed that people aren't quite sure of—they're not sure whether it contradicts the national or state constitution. When that happens, the law is usually tested in court to determine its "constitutionality"—that is, to find out whether it is unconstitutional. This is often done by having someone deliberately break the law and then stand trial. Lawyers for each side present arguments to try to show whether the law does or doesn't contradict the constitution, and a judge or jury listens to the arguments and decides which side has proved its case. The lawyers defending the law are mainly public officials, such as a state's attorney, and those against the law are hired by the people who wish to see the law tested. If it is decided that the law does not contradict the state or national constitution, it stays in effect and must be obeyed. If it is decided that the law contradicts the constitution, it is abolished. (Only the U.S. Supreme Court can abolish a national law by declaring it unconstitutional, but a state supreme court can abolish a state law.) When the Butler Act became a law of Tennessee, no one had really paid much attention to whether or not it might contradict the state or national constitution.

In fact, no one at first paid much attention to it at all. Most Tennessee newspapers didn't even mention it. However, one paper did run a small story headed: "Tennessee Bans the Teaching of Evolution." A few days later, that heading was noticed by a woman in an office in New York City, whose job was to read newspapers and look for just such headings. She was the executive secretary of the organization known as the American Civil Liberties Union, or ACLU.

The ACLU had been formed in 1920 by several men who strongly believed there should be an independent organization to provide free lawyers and legal help to defend the rights and freedom of any person or group in the United States that might be too poor, too ignorant—or too hated—to get a lawyer or legal help anywhere else. If it seemed to the ACLU that someone had been denied the right of freedom of speech, religion, or any of the other guaranteed freedoms, the ACLU would take that person's side. If it seemed as if a law had been passed somewhere that was contrary to the Bill of Rights of the United States Constitution, the ACLU would try to do something about it. The ACLU was not always—and still isn't—a very popular organization because many people have felt it sometimes defended persons, groups, or ideas that didn't deserve to be defended, and interfered with laws that should be passed, which might have been true in some situations.

At any rate, when the directors of the ACLU read the newspaper story about the new Tennessee law, they decided that the law probably contradicted the constitutional rights of freedom of speech and religion and should be tested in court. The ACLU sent a statement to all Tennessee newspapers, indicating that it would pay for all lawyers and cover all of the costs for any Tennessee teacher who was willing to become the defendant in a trial to test the constitutionality of the Butler Act. On May 4, 1925, one of Tennessee's major newspapers, the Chattanooga *Daily Times*, ran a story about the ACLU offer under the heading "Plan Assault on State Law on Evolution—Civil Liberties Union to File Test Case."

On the afternoon of the next day, Mr. Walter White, who was superintendent of schools in Rhea County, Tennessee, made a visit to a law office in the little town of Dayton, in Rhea County. The office belonged to two lawyers who were brothers, Herbert and Sue Hicks (Sue had been named for his mother, who had died giving birth to him). Mr. White asked the lawyers, both of whom he knew well, what they thought about the new anti-evolution law. Sue Hicks advised him not to pay any attention to it, inasmuch as no one would know what it meant until it was tested in court. Neither he, his brother, nor Mr. White had seen the story in the *Daily Times* the day before, but Hicks knew that the law was bound to be tested in court by somebody.

It was a very warm day, and Mr. White and Sue Hicks decided to walk over to the Robinson Drug Store and have a cooling glass of Coca-Cola at the soda fountain there. As they were sitting and sipping their drinks, another Dayton citizen came into the drugstore, saw them, and came to join them. He was George Rappelyea, local manager of the Cumberland Coal and Iron Company in Dayton. He, White, and Sue Hicks were all acquainted.

They chatted, and after a time the subject of the new law came up. Rappelyea, who had a degree as a doctor of mining engineering and had thus studied some geology and other sciences, believed firmly in evolution and was angered by the law. White, on the other hand, was a Fundamentalist; he favored the law because he was against exposing young people to anything that might undermine their faith in religion, which he felt the teaching of evolution did. Hicks wasn't a Fundamentalist, but from what he knew of evolution he didn't think it had really been proved.

As the three men argued their points of view, Frank Earle Robinson, the owner of the drugstore, came over to listen. Another man entered the store and, hearing the subject of the conversation, also came over to listen to what was being said. His name was Wallace Haggard, and coincidentally, he, like Hicks, was a lawyer.

After a time, Rappelyea happened to mention the story that had appeared in the *Daily Times* announcing the

ACLU's offer to test the law. As the men discussed this, Rappelyea came up with an idea: why not take advantage of the ACLU offer and have the court test held in Dayton? A trial would draw attention to the little town, bring in visitors, and help business. It could be a great thing for Dayton!

Sue Hicks was excited by the idea. So was Frank Robinson, who was a prominent member of an organization called the Dayton Progressive Club and was all for anything that could boost the town's prestige. The question came up of who could be found to volunteer to let himself or herself be accused of breaking the law. A few names were mentioned, and then someone suggested John Scopes, a young man who taught science and coached football at the Dayton high school. He wasn't married, so he didn't have a family to worry about. He was well liked, so he wouldn't run a risk of hostility from the Dayton Fundamentalists—they'd all understand he was doing it mainly to help the town, anyway. Besides, he really didn't have anything to lose: however the trial came out, he would still have his job, and the ACLU would pay all of his costs, win or lose.

Scopes was sent for and soon showed up; he was a nice-looking, quiet-spoken young man of twenty-four. Rappelyea and the others explained what they were up to and asked him if he might not have broken the new law. Scopes answered that probably every teacher in the state was breaking the law because the very biology textbook that was being used in most high schools, furnished by the State of Tennessee itself, discussed evolution quite thoroughly and even had Charles Darwin's picture in it!

The older men talked Scopes into agreeing to be the defendant in the test case. It was suggested that Sue and Herbert Hicks and Wallace Haggard could be the prosecuting attorneys (the lawyers who would attempt to show that the anti-evolution law was not unconstitutional and that Scopes had broken it), and John Godsey, an elderly ex-judge then working as a lawyer in Dayton, could be Scopes's defense attorney, with the job of proving the law unconstitutional and Scopes not guilty. Rappelyea wrote out a brief message to the ACLU, informing its directors that a volunteer for their test case had been found in Dayton, and rushed out to the nearest telegraph office to have the message sent as a telegram to New York (a long distance phone call from Dayton to New York wasn't possible in 1925, but a telegram would arrive the same day it was sent). A phone call was made to the *Daily Times*, in the nearby city of Chattanooga, to let the editors know that the test case for the Butler Act would be held in Dayton.

The next day a small story announcing that the trial was to be in Dayton appeared in the Chattanooga newspaper. A telegram also arrived from the ACLU, addressed to Rappelyea, agreeing to help with the trial as promised, offering several suggestions, and also offering to pay for the prosecution lawyers as well as for the defense. Rappelyea hurried to Robinson's drugstore, where some of the other "conspirators" were gathered and the rest soon arrived. With the help of Sue Hicks, Rappelyea wrote out a warrant for the arrest of John Scopes. Scopes himself, probably thinking it great fun, volunteered to find the sheriff or someone else who could legally arrest him. He went out and shortly returned with a man named Perry Swafford, who was a sheriff's deputy. Rappelyea handed the warrant to Swafford, who formally instructed Scopes to appear before the justices of the peace on the coming Saturday so that all necessary legal procedures could be taken care of and a date would be set for the trial. There was probably a good deal of joshing and bantering among the men, for after all, they were all in the "plot" together.

None of the men could possibly have foreseen what was going to happen as a result of their actions, but they had just set the stage for what was going to be one of the most bitter, controversial, and widely discussed trials of the twentieth century.

3

THE CHAMPIONS COME FORTH: THE DEFENDING AND PROSECUTING ATTORNEYS

The men who set up the Scopes trial expected it to be a moderately small affair. Sue Hicks and the other young lawyers who were to be involved in it were excited because it would be far more interesting than the sort of law work they usually did—drawing up wills, settling land claims, and so on—but they didn't expect it to last long or get very complicated.

However, when word began to get out that a trial was going to be held to test the Tennessee anti-evolution law, it attracted the attention of a number of men for whom the test was far more than just a minor trial in a small town. For these men, depending on their point of view, the trial would be a major battle between the forces of Fundamentalist Christianity and modern science, a confrontation between freedom of speech and suppression of thought, a struggle between Good and Evil! And these men wanted to be part of it. Both the prosecution and defense attorneys in Dayton suddenly found themselves receiving offers of volunteer help.

One of the first volunteers came in on the side of the defense. Judge Godsey, Scopes's sole defense attorney, spoke about the trial to a friend of his, John R. Neal, who was the head of a law school in Knoxville, the third largest city in Tennessee. Neal had been dean of the School of Law of the University of Tennessee and was considered to be the best lawyer in the state on any matters involving the constitution. He didn't claim to know much about evolution, but he was a firm believer in academic freedom—the right of teachers and students to study and discuss any legitimate educational subject and the right of a school to determine for itself what it would teach. Neal felt that the anti-evolution law violated academic freedom, so he wanted to help defend John Scopes. Scopes and Godsey were happy to have him, and Neal immediately went to work at his specialty, checking out the constitutionality of the anti-evolution law.

Few people outside Tennessee knew of John Neal, but the next volunteer to become part of the trial, on the side of the prosecution this time, was a man whose name was known to almost everyone in the United States. He was William Jennings Bryan, one of the leaders of the Democratic party, who had been a congressman and secretary of state and had been nominated three times to run for the highest office in the land, the presidency of the United States. Admired and respected by millions of people who shared his views—and hated by millions of others who did not—he played a role much like the one Senator Edward Kennedy was to play in the 1980s; although never elected president, Bryan shaped many of the programs and platforms of the Democratic party, and his ideas were listened to carefully by the party's other leaders. He was known as a defender of the "common" people—farmers, office and factory workers, shop owners, miners—against big business and banking interests. Because of this his followers had nicknamed him "The Great Commoner" and "The Peerless Leader" (this was a play on words, meaning that not only was he a leader without peer, or equal, but also that he was leader of the peer-less, or common people). Some of the things he supported and fought for were the right of women to vote (which they were not permitted to do until 1920); a government insurance fund to protect bank depositors; a Department of Labor in the U.S. Government, to protect the rights of working people; an income tax levied mainly on the wealthy, to provide money for programs to aid the poor and needy; and the election of senators by the *people* of their states, rather than just by politicians in the state legislatures, as was once done. These, of course, are all things that we now have today, and Bryan helped achieve them. He also backed some controversial and unpopular ideas, such as Prohibition, the law that made it illegal for anyone to buy beer, wine, or any other alcoholic beverage in the United States from 1920 to 1933. Most historians of today agree that William Jennings Bryan was a sincere, honorable man who believed firmly in trying to do things for the good of the common people. Politically, he was a liberal, meaning one who is in favor of progress and of having government make changes to benefit people. However, it appears that Bryan was not a very deep thinker. Apparently, he would form opinions about things he did not understand very well, or didn't understand at all, and never bother to try to find out if his opinion was valid or not.

In 1925, Bryan was sixty-five years old, and his long, illustrious political career was just about over. But he had always been a spellbinding speechmaker, who could sway the opinions of people with his words. He still made speeches all over the country and wrote columns for the newspaper he owned, *The Commoner*. Now, however, more of his speeches and writings were concerned with religion than with politics. Bryan was a deeply religious man, an official of the Presbyterian church, and for several years he had been growing more and more concerned about the conflict between religion and the subject of evolution. He believed that the Bible story of creation was the truth and that the evolution theory was wrong, and in time he came to believe that the teaching of evolution was actually dangerous. It seemed to him that the teaching of evolution had been a major cause of World War I because, he felt, there was evidence that it had been the Darwinian idea of "survival of the fittest" that had led the German nation to go to war. He also felt that the concept of survival of the fittest was causing the trouble that was taking place between workers and employers during the early 1920s, a time of many strikes and much violence. It angered him that belief in evolution had caused "modern-ization" to creep into many Protestant denominations so that they no longer believed in much of the Old Testament of the Bible and that the teaching of evolution was causing many young people in high schools and colleges to cast aside belief in the Bible in favor of modern scientific attitudes. And so Bryan had begun a "crusade" against the teaching of evolution, just as he had crusaded against big business and other targets during his political career. One of his most frequently given lectures was titled "The Men-ace of Darwinism," with which he tried to alert people to what he regarded as the danger of allowing evolution to be taught in the nation's schools.

In his speeches and writings, he attacked Modernist ministers and churches, as well as scientists, whom he referred to as "dishonest scoundrels" who were "stealing away the faith of your children." With what appeared to be contempt for scientific discoveries, he declared, "It is bet-ter to trust in the Rock of Ages [religion] than to know the age of rocks; it is better for one to know that he is close to the Heavenly Father than to know how far the stars in the heavens are apart!" It was actually Bryan who was the guiding spirit behind the Fundamentalist efforts to have anti-evolution bills passed in several of the southern states; he was well acquainted with many of the politicians in state legislatures, and it was often he who urged them to introduce anti-evolution bills and gather votes to get them passed. In an exuberant letter to a Fundamentalist friend he wrote, "The movement will sweep the country and we will drive Darwinism from our schools."

Bryan was traveling around the country making anti-evolution speeches when he heard about the Scopes trial. He made a statement, which of course was reported in newspapers, that he would like to help with the prosecution of the case, at his own expense. He was a graduate of a law school and had been a lawyer as a young man, before getting into politics, so he was qualified to act as an attorney.

The Hicks brothers, Rappelyea, and the rest of the little group of Dayton "conspirators" were delighted to hear of Bryan's offer because the presence of such a famous man at the trial would be worth a tremendous amount of publicity, which was sure to focus the attention of the whole nation on the trial and the town. The Hicks brothers sent Bryan a letter assuring him that, "We will consider it a great honor to have you with us in this prosecution." Thus, William Jennings Bryan, "The Great Commoner" (known to those who disliked him as "The Great Windbag") became one of the attorneys for the prosecution of John Scopes.

This news hit the front pages of the nation's newspapers with a splash, and, almost immediately, John Scopes's defense attorneys, Godsey and Neal, heard from two volunteers who wanted to help *their* side in the trial. One of these was Dudley Malone, a successful lawyer who, like Bryan, was prominent in Democratic party politics. He had, in fact, been assistant secretary of state in the administration of President Woodrow Wilson (1913–1920) at the same time Bryan had been secretary of state, staunchly backing many of the things Bryan had crusaded for, such as the right of women to vote. He was a liberal, just as Bryan was, and so he was an ardent believer in freedom of speech, academic freedom, and other principles he felt the Tennessee anti-evolution law was trampling on. As far as religion was concerned, he was a Catholic who attended church only infrequently and who did not believe the Bible was necessarily accurate in all matters. He had no particular opinion on evolution.

Malone was nowhere nearly as well known as William Jennings Bryan, but the other man who accompanied Malone as a volunteer was. He was Clarence Darrow, the most famous trial lawyer in America, a man renowned for his ability to dig facts out of witnesses with his questioning and to bring juries to his side with his marvelous speeches. At the time he offered his services to Scopes, Darrow was sixty-eight years old, three years older than Bryan, and his name had been appearing in the newspapers for thirty years.

Darrow first gained the attention of the nation when he quit a high-paying job as a lawyer for a railroad company to act as attorney for the head of the Railway Workers Union, Eugene V. Debs, who was charged with causing violence and destruction in a strike against the railroads. Debs had been portrayed by the newspapers as a viciously dangerous man who was seeking to wreck the entire nation, and he was being tried for criminal conspiracy, a very serious charge that could have put him in prison for many years. People wondered why a successful lawyer would want to defend such a man.

But Darrow brought out, for the nation to see, the dreadful working conditions and poor pay of many workers in the railroad industry, showed how Debs had spent his life honorably and legally working to improve such conditions, and showed how the managers of the railroads had actually broken the law themselves in a number of ways, virtually "framing" Debs. When Darrow announced that he intended to have these men called onto the witness stand to be questioned by him, the trial was quickly halted on a technicality, the criminal conspiracy charges against Debs were allowed to simply fade away, and Debs had to serve only a six-month sentence for failing to obey a government order to halt the strike. Technically, Darrow had lost the case, but Debs had really been saved from severe punishment. The effort of the railroads to smash the union had been thwarted, and a great many people had become aware that Clarence Darrow was a brilliant thinker and marvelous speaker, who cared very deeply and sincerely about the problems of common working people. Eventually, he was hired as an attorney by a number of labor unions, which at that time in history were struggling to gain for workers the rights and benefits that are taken for granted today, such as an eight-hour workday, and the right to even belong to a union. In some of the cases that Darrow handled for labor unions he won impressive victories.

Darrow became known as a man who was willing to defend poor, desperate, downtrodden people. He hated injustice, oppression, and indifference to suffering. At that time, because of racial prejudice, it was almost impossible for an African-American to find a white lawyer who would defend him or her even for payment, but Darrow acted as the attorney for a number of black people, often helping them financially as well. He felt they were the "underdogs under the underdogs" of the United States, and he sympathized with their plight.

At times, his viewpoint caused Darrow trouble because he frequently defended people that millions of

Americans felt did not deserve to be defended—conscientious objectors, men who had refused to serve in the armed forces of the United States during World War I, and Communists accused of plotting revolution. In one of his most famous cases, he even defended two wealthy young men who had confessed to a horrible, senseless murder, and he had managed to save them from the death penalty. But Darrow did not care if his defense of such cases angered people; he believed that the same law existed for everyone—rich and poor—and he would not turn down a plea for help.

Darrow stood for many of the same things William Jennings Bryan did, and in fact, he had campaigned for Bryan when Bryan first ran for president. But in one major respect, Darrow was completely different: whereas Bryan was deeply religious, Darrow was an avowed agnostic (one who feels it is impossible to know whether there is or isn't a God). Although he was friends with many clergymen, Darrow felt that religion was all too often narrow-minded and intent on keeping people ignorant and obedient. He was quite disturbed about the Fundamentalist movement, fearing that the Fundamentalists were trying to force their particular kind of religion on the entire country. For Darrow, the Scopes trial offered a chance to make people aware of what he believed was the Fundamentalist threat to both religious freedom and the freedom of American schools to teach scientifically established fact rather than mere rigid belief in the Bible.

John Scopes and attorney John Neal consulted with the American Civil Liberties Union, and it was agreed to let Darrow and Malone become part of the Scopes defense team. The ACLU also contributed one of its own lawyers, forty-three-year-old Arthur Garfield Hays, an attorney who was an expert on all of the little formal, technical matters involved in conducting a trial. Hays was Jewish but did not follow traditional Jewish religion and accepted evolution as a fact.

So the final team that would defend Scopes and try to get the anti-evolution law repealed consisted of Clarence Darrow, Dudley Malone, Arthur Hays, John Neal, and Neal's law partner, a young man named F. B. McElwee. Judge Godsey, who had been Scopes's first defense attorney, had taken himself out of the picture. Practically a Fundamentalist himself, he was worried about what other Fundamentalists might think of him for working against the antievolution law. He later even made a public apology to the people of Dayton for ever having associated with such men as the agnostic Darrow and the other liberals of the defense team.

For the prosecution, the final team that was put together included the Hicks brothers, Wallace Haggard, and two other local lawyers: Ben G. McKenzie, a former assistant attorney general, and his son, J. Gordon McKenzie, a former judge. William Jennings Bryan had asked that his lawyer son, William Jennings Bryan, Jr., be added to the group; and his request was, of course, granted. The prosecution was headed by A. Thomas Stewart, attorney general for the 18th Judicial Circuit of Tennessee, a man in his mid-thirties. Several of these men were ardent Fundamentalists, while others ranged from deeply to moderately religious.

But for all of the millions of people now reading about the trial in their newspapers, most of these lawyers were merely "extras," like the "extras" in a movie. The "stars" were Bryan and Darrow. Even if it had been conducted by unknown country lawyers, the Scopes trial would have been of moderate interest to some people—teachers, scientists, and intellectuals on one side and followers of Fundamentalism on the other—simply because of what was involved. Its outcome would probably have been reported on the second or third page of most newspapers. But now that two of the most famous personalities of the period, both known as marvelously skillful orators, had taken sides and were to be pitted against each other, the trial assumed front-page importance, and everything that happened in it was destined to be covered by the nation's media. If there had been television in 1925, there would have been plans to have the Scopes trial covered by every channel and beamed throughout the world.

4

THE "MONKEY TRIAL" BEGINS

Dayton, Tennessee, is in the southeastern part of the state. In 1925 it had a population of 1,700–1,800 citizens, all of whom belonged to some Protestant denomination—there were no Catholics, Jews, or any other religious minority in the town. Many Daytonians were Fundamentalists, but many others were not, and there were even some that apparently leaned in favor of evolution.

Most of the leading people of Dayton hoped that the Scopes trial would attract a good number of visitors and perhaps some new residents, even some new businesses. They expected that as many as forty thousand people might visit the town during the days of the trial. Colored flags and banners were hung along Main Street, and a number of wooden refreshment stands selling sandwiches, hot dogs, soft drinks, and ice cream (the hamburger had not yet become commonplace in the United States) were erected on Main and other streets. Because most people were under the impression that evolution taught that humans had descended from monkeys, the nation's newspapers were calling the event "The Monkey Trial." To go along with that theme, many local merchants put cardboard monkeys in the windows of their stores, and there were stuffed toy monkeys for sale as well as large pin-on buttons that bore the words "Your Old Man's a Monkey"— souvenirs for visitors to take home as mementos of the event.

Many Daytonians were annoyed by this carnival-like atmosphere, but they hadn't seen anything yet. As the day for the trial to begin drew close, swarms of reporters from every major newspaper in the country descended on the town, along with a team of engineers and announcers from radio station WGN in Chicago (Darrow's hometown) and a number of motion picture cameramen from Hollywood, sent by the film studios to make what were known as "newsreels" (all-news films) of the trial. There were even British, French, and German reporters present to cover the trial. There was no Fundamentalist movement in Europe, and Europeans were astonished that a trial such as this, to defend a scientifically accepted subject from religious attack, could take place in a civilized, progressive nation in the twentieth century. An English reporter, talking to a member of the Scopes defense group, is said to have remarked, "Whole blooming thing is quite fantastic, don't you know? Can't quite credit my senses."

Farm families began coming in from the surrounding countryside for miles around, and mountaineers came down out of the hills that rose beyond Dayton. These were people for whom religion was the most important thing in their lives, and they had come to watch the champions of Christianity cast down the devil-inspired atheists and scientists who were trying to corrupt their children. Many were self-appointed preachers, who stood on corners, singing hymns and urging passersby to be saved. They slept in the horse-drawn wagons they had driven in, or pitched tents in the parks, or simply curled up under trees.

Peddlers selling Bibles and other religious items, show-men, bands of musicians, and a variety of wild-eyed "holy men," with titles such as "John the Baptist the Third" and "Deck Carter, Bible Champion of the World," drifted into the town. Huge signs, produced by a Fundamentalist sign painter, appeared on utility poles, trees, and the fronts of buildings, offering such messages as "You Need God in Your Business" and "Read Your Bible Daily for One Week." A couple of "professional atheists" showed up, apparently to see what kind of reaction they could get, and several circus performers with trained chimpanzees arrived, hoping to cash in on the "Monkey Trial" theme (although chimpanzees are apes, not monkeys). By sheer coincidence, during the week of the trial, there was a convention of the fanatical Christian sect known as "holy rollers" in the area, and the faint sound of their howls, as they threshed and rolled in religious frenzy during their meetings out in the hills, drifted through the town at night. To the horror of its citizens, Dayton seemed to have become a combination carnival, revival meeting, and worldwide media event!

The jurors for the trial were selected on Friday, July 10, 1925, and the trial opened the following Monday morning, in sweltering southern heat. The Dayton courthouse seated seven hundred people, and there were an additional three hundred standing wherever they could, so the packed room was like an oven. Many people cooled themselves with big fans made from palm leaves, a common sight in those days before air conditioning, when even electric fans were rare.

The indictment (formal accusation of a crime) of Scopes was read by Attorney General A. Thomas Stewart, the head of the prosecution. It stated, in general, that John Scopes had "unlawfully" but "willfully" taught in school "a certain theory and theories that deny the story of the Divine Creation as taught in the Bible, and did teach instead thereof that man has descended from a lower order of animals." Judge John Raulston, of Dayton, asked the defense attorneys how they pleaded to the charge.

John Neal arose and stated that the defense moved to quash (cancel) the indictment on the basis that it violated the state constitution of Tennessee on thirteen counts. This meant it was now up to the judge to decide whether or not to quash the indictment, and he would make that decision by listening to arguments from both sides. The defense would have to convince him that the indictment violated the constitution; the prosecution would have to prove that it did not. If Raulston decided to quash the indictment, it would mean he was ruling that the Butler Act was unconstitutional; and in order to keep the law from being abolished, the prosecution would have to make an appeal to take the case to a higher court, the Supreme Court of Tennessee.

Because this was a matter that involved only the judge's decision, not the jury's, the members of the jury were sent out of the courtroom so that they wouldn't hear anything that might prejudice them toward one side or the other if the trial continued. The arguments then began, with John Neal giving a rundown of the thirteen points that the defense attorneys believed made the law unconstitutional. The main ones were that there was an article in the Tennessee constitution stating that "it shall be the duty of the general assembly to cherish literature and science" and that the law violated this article by attacking science rather than cherishing it; that the law also violated an article stating that "no preference shall be given to any religious establishment or mode of worship" because it made specific reference to the Christian Bible; that it violated an article stating that "every citizen may freely speak, write, and print on any subject"; and that it violated an article requiring that no bill could become law if it dealt with more than one subject, whereas this law was so vaguely worded that it dealt with two subjects—the teaching of evolution *and* the teaching of the Bible. The other points were minor. Arthur Garfield Hays and Dudley Malone presented specific arguments for the main points.

The prosecution then took up its arguments. Ben McKenzie answered the charge that the law was vaguely worded by insisting that every citizen of Tennessee understood its meaning perfectly. Sue Hicks answered the charge involving freedom of speech by arguing that a teacher had to teach what he or she was *hired* to teach and thus could not, for example, claim freedom of speech to teach architecture when he or she had been hired to teach mathematics. A. Thomas Stewart denied the charge against violation of freedom of religion by insisting that inasmuch as the Bible was recognized throughout the nation, no preference was being given to one religion over another by having the law refer to the Bible. However, this showed that by "religion" Stewart was speaking only of Christian denominations that used the Bible.

"Does it [the law] not prefer the Bible over the Koran?" Dudley Malone challenged him. The Koran is the holy book of the Islamic religion, and Malone was making the point that by mentioning only the Bible, the law was giving preference to Christianity over Islam and other minority religions.

"We are not living in a heathen country," replied Stewart. By this, he apparently meant that inasmuch as the United States was mainly a Christian country and not an Islamic one, such as Saudi Arabia or Egypt, the Bible *should* have preference over the Koran, in the eyes of the law.

Clarence Darrow made the final argument for the day,

a kind of summing-up of the defense's point of view. As he got up to speak, a man in the audience growled, "I'd like to hear this man talk for ten minutes and then hang him!"

Darrow began by trying to show how, in the defense's opinion, the anti-evolution law violated religious freedom. He pointed out that there were "intelligent, scholarly Christians, who by the millions throughout the United States, find no inconsistency [disagreement] between evolution and religion," and he charged that their religious beliefs were thus being attacked by this law that insisted there was *no* meeting ground between evolution and religion. He reminded the judge that there were many such people in Tennessee, people who "believed that organic life and the plants and animals and man . . . are the subjects of evolution." Then, he asserted, along came the Fundamentalists, insisting that everyone had to believe as they believe, passing a law making it a criminal offense to teach any origin of man that was "in conflict with the divine account in the Bible." He snarled that they had no more right to single out the Bible as a divine book than the Koran or the Book of Mormon or the writings of Confucius or Buddha—a suggestion that the rights of minority religions were also being violated.

Darrow protested against using the Bible as a measure for teaching science. "What *is* the Bible?" he asked, and went on to explain what serious scholars had found out about it. "The Bible is made up of sixty-six books written over a period of about one thousand years, some of them very early and some of them comparatively late. It is a book of religion and morals. It is not a book of science. Never was and never was meant to be." Some of the people in the audience, mostly farmers and mountaineers, began to leave. Perhaps they refused to listen to what Darrow was saying about the Bible, or perhaps they were simply bored. Ignoring them, Darrow went on. "It is not a book on geology," he told the audience. "Its authors knew nothing about geology. It is not a book on biology, they knew nothing about it. . . ." He pointed out that the authors of the Bible had believed in many things now known to be incorrect, such as that the earth was the center of the universe and that the sun went around *it*. "We know better," he reminded his listeners.

He charged that the law was inconsistent because it made the teaching of evolution in public schools a criminal act—a crime—but said nothing at all about private schools. But a criminal law had to be equally applied, he insisted. It must apply to *all*. You can't call a man a criminal for teaching evolution in a public school while the man who teaches it in a private school is innocent under the law, Darrow thundered. You can't make it a crime for a man to teach evolution in a school when books teaching evolution can be bought in almost every bookstore in the state, he argued.

But Darrow indicated that he felt the law for public schools was just the beginning. "If today you can take a thing like evolution and make it a crime to teach it in the public school, tomorrow you can make it a crime to teach it in the private school," he warned. "Today it is the public school teachers, tomorrow, the private. The next day, the preachers and lecturers, the magazines, the books, the newspapers—." Flinging up his hands, he roared that the law could start the nation marching backward to the darkness of the Middle Ages, when fanatics had lighted fires "to burn the men who dared bring any intelligence and enlightenment [truth and knowledge] and culture to the human mind!"

Part of Darrow's argument was shrewd legal point-making, and part was sheer dramatic speech making, but most of the people who heard it apparently found it very effective. Later, after the trial was halted for the day, one of

Darrow's opponents, prosecution attorney Ben McKenzie, came up to Darrow, put an arm around his shoulders, and told him, "It was the greatest speech I ever heard in my life on any subject." Several Daytonians passing him on the street as he walked back to his hotel murmured, "A wonderful speech, Mr. Darrow," and one man stopped him to ask for a handshake. However, while Darrow had been making his speech, a woman in the courtroom, presumably a Fundamentalist, was heard to snarl out the words, "The damned *infidel* [a person who does not believe in religion]!" Obviously, Darrow's views were rejected by many, no matter how fine his speech might have been.

But from the defense viewpoint the important thing was, had the speech helped influence Judge Raulston? If he ruled in favor of the defense, to quash the indictment, the trial would be over, the anti-evolution law would be ruled unconstitutional, and the Fundamentalist cause would be dealt a serious setback.

5

MOVES AND COUNTERMOVES

Darrow's speech was given on Monday afternoon, and Judge Raulston intended to announce his decision on Tuesday afternoon. But around noon on Tuesday, all of the newspapers of one of the nation's largest newspaper chains came out with a story that Raulston had decided to rule against the motion to quash, and the trial would go on. Things were held up while Raulston angrily tried to discover how the papers had gained this information. He was embarrassed to learn that he had accidentally revealed his intentions to one of the chain's reporters.

So it was no surprise when, on Wednesday morning, Raulston ruled against quashing the indictment. Darrow was unsurprised but bitter. Raulston was a deeply religious man who insisted, against the defense attorneys' protests, on starting each day of trial with a prayer by a clergyman, although this was not standard procedure in United States courthouses. Apparently, Darrow would have been surprised *had* such a man ruled against a law supporting the Bible.

So the trial would continue. Judge Raulston asked the

defense attorneys how they now pleaded. "Not guilty," answered John Neal.

A selected lawyer for each side then presented his side's definition of the case. The prosecution's argument was simply that John Scopes had broken the law by teaching something he wasn't supposed to teach. The defense's viewpoint, carefully worked out by the defense attorneys and presented by Dudley Malone, was that the wording of the law actually caused Scopes to be accused of two separate acts—teaching a theory that denied the biblical account of the creation *and* teaching that humans were descended from a lower order of animals. Therefore, the defense insisted that the prosecution would have to show that Scopes had not only taught about evolution but had also actually taught that evolution contradicted the biblical story of creation. The defense maintained that he could not have done so because, as they intended to show, there was *no* contradiction. "We shall show," said Malone "that there are millions of people who believe in evolution *and* in the stories of creation as set forth in the Bible, and who find no conflict between the two."

But Malone then revealed that the defense had more in mind than simply to have Scopes found not guilty. "The narrow purpose of the defense is to establish the innocence of the defendant Scopes," he stated. "The broad purpose of the defense will be to prove that the Bible is a work of religious aspirations [hope for betterment] and rules of conduct which must be kept in the field of theology [religious study]. The defense maintains that there is no more justification for imposing the conflicting views of the Bible on courses of biology than there would be for imposing the views of biologists on courses of comparative religion. We maintain that science and religion embrace two separate and distinct fields of thought and learning." Thus, Malone made it plain that the main purpose of the

The English naturalist Charles Darwin revolutionized people's thinking about their origins with his theory of evolution by natural selection. His famous book, published over 130 years ago, aroused a storm of controversy that continues to this day.

ON

THE ORIGIN OF SPECIES

BY MEANS OF NATURAL SELECTION,

OR THE

PRESERVATION OF FAVOURED RACES IN THE STRUGGLE
FOR LIFE.

By CHARLES DARWIN, M.A.,
FELLOW OF THE ROYAL, GEOLOGICAL, LINNÆAN, ETC., SOCIETIES;
AUTHOR OF ' JOURNAL OF RESEARCHES DURING H. M. S. BEAGLE'S VOYAGE
ROUND THE WORLD.'

LONDON:
JOHN MURRAY, ALBEMARLE STREET.
1859.
p. x°.

The right of Translation is reserved.

Human evolution
is ridiculed in this
1872 cartoon showing
a human's descent from
pig to bull to man.

Lucille Milner alerted the
American Civil Liberties
Union to a newspaper story
announcing that the state
of Tennessee had banned
the teaching of evolution.

The original Robinson's Drug Store on Main Street in Dayton, Tennessee, where the Scopes Trial was planned.

The drugstore's owner, Frank Earle Robinson (standing), discusses the trial with his friends (left to right) George Rappelyea, Walter White, and Clay Green.

The Fundamentalists had plenty of anti-evolution
literature to share with the thousands of visitors
who came to Dayton to witness the trial.

William Jennings Bryan

Clarence Darrow (right) speaks with Ben G. McKenzie, a lawyer for the prosecution, during the trial. (Below) Three key men in the Scopes defense team (left to right): Dudley Malone, John Neal, and Clarence Darrow.

The twenty-four-year-old defendant, John Scopes, is
flanked by Malone (left) and Darrow.

Judge John F. Raulston presided over the trial,
expecting it to last one day. To his amazement,
the trial lasted ten days and drew worldwide
attention. (Facing page) Eleven of the dozen men
who formed the jury for the Scopes trial, flanked here
by Judge Raulston on the right and an unidentified
man on the left; and a view of the courtroom.

John Scopes's students are sworn in before they testified that their teacher taught them information about the origins of humans other than what Tennessee law allowed. One of the young men, when asked whether or not a whale was a mammal, thought the question was a joke.

Dudley Malone leans over to talk with the defendant, seated here with his father, Thomas Scopes, Sr. Arthur Hayes, a lawyer for the ACLU, stands behind them.

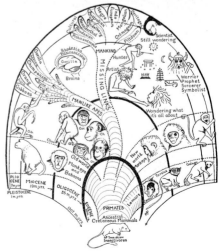

William Jennings Bryan
delivers his first speech,
in which he ridiculed
several diagrams found in
Scopes's high school biology
textbook, similar to the
one shown at right.

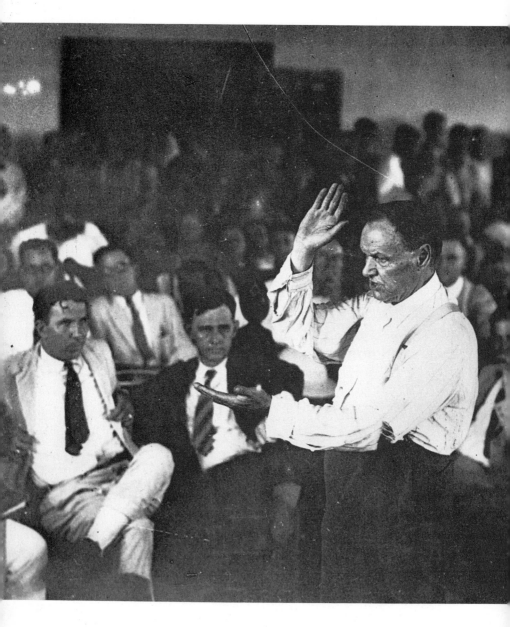

Darrow in action during the trial

At one point the trial was moved outdoors, where
many of the spectators sat on hard wooden benches.
It was here where Darrow gave Bryan a grueling
interrogation on the witness stand.

(Top) Darrow and Bryan (with fan) chat during
a recess in the trial. (Bottom) Darrow received
stacks of mail from all over the
country while the trial was in progress.

John Scopes (center, white shirt) stands before
the bar for sentencing. The jury found him
guilty of violating the state law and the
judge imposed upon him a fine of $100.

A man dressed up in a gorilla suit stages a sit-in demonstration outside the post office building in Little Rock, Arkansas, where a court trial challenging an Arkansas law that requires schools to teach scientific creationism is in session.

In most states, public school students can study biology textbooks that teach Darwin's theory of evolution.

trial would be to attempt to stop the Fundamentalist effort to have their religious viewpoint taught in public schools in place of accepted scientific knowledge.

It was now time for the calling of witnesses, with the prosecution calling its witnesses first. There were only a few of them. Walter White, the superintendent of Rhea County schools, came to the stand and, under questioning by A. Thomas Stewart, indicated that Scopes had admitted, during the conversation in Robinson's drugstore back in May, that he had taught evolution to his high school classes. Two of Scopes's students, boys in their teens, testified under questioning that Scopes had indeed discussed evolution in class. Shortly afterward, having established without a doubt that Scopes had definitely taught evolution in defiance of the law, the state rested its case (called no more witnesses).

Then it was the defense's turn. Their first witness was Dr. Maynard Metcalf, a research professor of zoology at Johns Hopkins University and a member in good standing of the Congregationalist church. For some reason, as Metcalf was seating himself in the witness chair, William Jennings Bryan rose, came over to stand in front of the scientist, glared down at him for a few moments, then shuffled silently back to his place among the prosecution attorneys.

Questioned by Clarence Darrow, Dr. Metcalf vigorously acknowledged that he believed in evolution. Darrow asked him if it wasn't true that practically *all* of the world's scientists were evolutionists. Metcalf's answer was "I am acquainted with practically all of the zoologists, botanists, and geologists of this country—I know there is not a single one among them that doubts the fact of evolution." He went on, under questioning, to explain that although evolution was regarded as a fact, there were a number of theories to account for it—to scientists, "theory" meant "logical explanation," not "guess," as Fundamentalists seemed to believe. He gave some examples of the evidence for evolution.

When Metcalf was finished, Clarence Darrow made it plain, in a short statement to Judge Raulston, that Metcalf was only the first of a number of similar witnesses who had come to Dayton to testify for the defense. These included not only scientists who were both firm believers in evolution and faithful members of Christian churches but also ministers of several Christian denominations that fully accepted evolution as the work of God. The defense intended to show that evolution was a fact that deserved to be taught in American schools and that it was not actually in conflict with Christianity.

However, Attorney General Stewart announced that the prosecution objected to the testimony of such witnesses on the grounds that the purpose of the trial was not to determine whether or not evolution was true and acceptable but simply to determine whether or not Scopes had broken the law by teaching it. This meant that once again Judge Raulston was going to have to make a decision. He was going to have to decide whether or not scientists and ministers could be called as witnesses for the defense, and again he was going to have to make his decision on the basis of arguments given by the attorneys on each side. And once more, because they were not to be involved and because the lawyers' arguments might prejudice them, the jury members were sent out of the courtroom.

The honor of making the first argument for the prosecution had been given to William Jennings Bryan, Jr., who turned out to be a far cry from the masterful speaker his father was. He did little more than repeat the attorney general's charge that the testimony of scientists and ministers had no bearing on whether or not Scopes was guilty of teaching evolution.

Arthur Hays answered this argument for the defense. How could the jury possibly decide whether or not Scopes was guilty of teaching evolution when most of them didn't even know precisely what evolution *was*, questioned Hays. That was the *purpose* of the scientific witnesses, he explained: to provide information about evolution. He also contended that there was, in fact, a good deal more involved in this trial than merely the guilt or innocence of Scopes. He pointed out that William Jennings Bryan had made speeches in which he referred to the trial as "a duel to the death" between science and religion, which indeed it was, and that was why scientists should be permitted to testify. "The eyes of the country, in fact of the whole world, are upon you here," he told Judge Raulston.

Prosecution attorney Herbert Hicks took the floor, insisting that scientific witnesses would actually be interfering with the jury's duty of making up its mind about evolution. There was some wrangling between the attorneys on both sides, and then, inasmuch as it was a quarter to twelve o'clock, Judge Raulston adjourned the trial until one thirty.

During the break, word leaked out that at the afternoon session the final argument for the prosecution would be given by William Jennings Bryan. Fundamentalists licked their chops and rubbed their hands in glee. This was the moment they had been waiting for. Now their great crusading leader would use his marvelous powers of oratory to flatten and bewilder Darrow and the other "atheistic" defense attorneys, to show that evolution was nothing but groundless nonsense, and to prove that the words of the Bible were the unyielding truth. They felt that the trial would soon be over.

6

A SETBACK
FOR THE
DEFENSE

Some people have said that when William Jennings Bryan walked forward to a spot in front of Judge Raulston's table to begin his speech, he was firm and erect. Others have said he appeared to be trembling, possibly the effect of strain and the dreadful heat on a man of his age. In one hand he held a big palm-leaf fan, which was almost a trademark for him whenever he spoke or lectured anywhere. He began to speak in a clear voice that carried to all parts of the courtroom. It was noteworthy, however, that although he was supposed to be addressing his arguments to Judge Raulston, he actually had his back to the judge most of the time, facing the audience. Obviously, he was speaking mainly to his Fundamentalist followers within the room.

He commented that he had not wished to take part in the discussion up to this point because it had seemed more fitting to let the lawyers who were residents of Tennessee do most of the talking for their state. But now, because matters had broadened out, because the defense wanted to bring in men from all parts of the country to testify, Bryan said he felt compelled to speak. The people of Tennessee had known what they were doing when they passed the anti-evolution law, he insisted; they knew the dangers of the "doctrine" of evolution and didn't want it taught to their children. And, he claimed, it wasn't proper to bring in outside "experts" to try to defeat their purpose.

He began to discuss the teaching of evolution, using the high school biology textbook that Scopes had used in teaching his classes as an example. He ridiculed many of the book's statements and diagrams, particularly one that included a drawing of a human within a circle of drawings of other animals of the class of mammals. How dare they put man in among all those smelly creatures, Bryan asked sarcastically, apparently implying that humans were not mammals. He drew some laughter with mocking remarks about certain aspects of evolution, as he understood it, such as that evolutionists weren't even willing to let Americans claim descent from "American monkeys" but had forced them to be descended from "Old World monkeys" instead. "Tell me that the parents of this day have not any right to declare that children are not to be taught this doctrine," he exclaimed, and he went on to insist that "the parents have a right to say that no teacher paid by their money shall rob their children of faith in God and send them back to their homes skeptical infidels, or agnostics, or atheists!" He angrily denounced evolutionists, charging that "they not only have no proof but they cannot find the beginning. . . . They do not talk about God!"

His voice rising, he declared that the Bible was "not going to be driven out of this court" by "experts" who had come hundreds of miles to try to show that evolution was not in conflict with the biblical story of Creation. Their only point in coming, he finished, was "to banish from the hearts of the people the Word of God as revealed!"

Bryan was still a marvelous speaker who knew how to use gestures, how to raise and lower his voice for dramatic effect, how to string words together in a powerful way. While he spoke, he truly had most of the audience hanging on his every word; and when he finished, he received loud applause. Clearly, the Fundamentalists present believed he had thoroughly demolished the opposition.

It is now known that Bryan was not really the 100 percent anti-evolutionist he made himself out to be. Shortly before the beginning of the Scopes Trial, he told a friend, Dr. Howard Kelly, that he really had no objection to the idea that evolution had affected every life form except humans, but he couldn't admit to this publicly. And in a conversation with the Hicks brothers during the trial, he said, "You boys will probably live to see whether or not evolution is true. I won't." He surely would not have said such a thing if he was as absolutely positive that evolution was wrong as he publicly insisted he was.

Dudley Malone presented the last argument of the day for the defense. He went back to the defense's main point that the prosecution not only had to prove that Scopes had taught evolution but would also have to prove that he had taught something that was in conflict with the story of creation in the Bible. Malone cried out that the defense had the right to produce witnesses who could show that Scopes had not done this because they would show that evolution was not in conflict with the Bible. "We have the right," he insisted, "to submit evidence to the court, of men . . . who are students of the Bible and authorities on the Bible and authorities on the scientific world." As Darrow had done, Malone challenged the use of the Bible as a means of teaching science. He thundered that the witnesses "have a right to testify in support of our view that the Bible is not to be taken literally as an authority in a court of science."

"Are we to hold mankind to a literal understanding [firm belief] of the claim that the world is six thousand years old because of the limited vision of men [the authors of the Bible] who believed the world was flat and that the earth was the center of the universe?" Malone demanded. "Are we to have our children know nothing about science except what the church says they shall know?"

As Malone spoke, in a voice that actually thundered throughout the room, the audience became more *excited* by his eloquence than they had been by Bryan's. His speech was punctuated with spatters of applause. People could be seen squirming excitedly in their chairs.

Glaring at the prosecution lawyers, Malone asked why they feared the testimony of the defense witnesses. Why does the prosecution fear, so greatly, the teaching of science, he wondered. "I would like to say something for the children of the country," he stated, looking back at Judge Raulston. "The least that this generation can do, Your Honor, is to give the next generation all the facts, with the hope that they will make a better world of this than *we* have been able to make of it!" In a pleading voice he cried out: "For God's sake, let the children have their minds kept open!"

Finally, Malone turned to look squarely at William Jennings Bryan. "We feel we stand with progress," he proclaimed. "We feel we stand with science. We feel we stand with intelligence. We feel we stand with fundamental freedom in America. We are not afraid." He turned back to Judge Raulston. "We ask Your Honor to admit the evidence [of the scientific experts] as a matter of correct law, as a matter of sound procedure, and as a matter of justice for the defense in this case!"

The courtroom broke into a thunder of applause that went on for nearly fifteen minutes. Malone had completely eclipsed the great Bryan's speech.

But the prosecution had the advantage of making the

last argument, presented by Attorney General Stewart, and he too made a passionate, powerful speech. He warned that if scientists were allowed to testify and to show that many people's ideas of the Bible were wrong, it would open the door to legal battles against all aspects of religion and the Bible "until finally, that precious book and its glorious teachings upon which this civilization has been built will be taken from us." He asked Judge Raulston not to allow the testimony of the scientists and other defense witnesses because "it would be a never-ending controversy"; and, in his opinion, testimony that did nothing to solve a problem, but only made it worse, was legally inadmissible (that is, should not be allowed).

When Stewart finished, Raulston banged his gavel and adjourned the trial for the day. Obviously, he was not yet ready to make his decision.

But he made it the next day, Friday, July 17. He began the day of trial by reading a statement he had prepared, explaining that he had decided that the purpose of the trial was simply to determine if John Scopes had broken the law and that neither science nor religion was involved in that matter. Therefore, neither scientists nor ministers were needed to testify, so he was denying the defense attorneys' request to let them appear as expert witnesses.

Thus, it looked as if the trial would soon be over, for without any witnesses to testify before the jury, the defense lawyers would not be able to do anything more than give their "closing" speeches, to try to persuade the jury of Scopes's innocence. However, it wasn't the defense's intention to let the end of the trial bring the whole matter to a close. Arthur Garfield Hays, the man who understood the importance of technicalities, leaped to his feet and got the leader of the prosecution, Attorney General Stewart, to agree that the defense was entitled to have a written record of the testimony that the witnesses would have given put into the records of the trial so that the testimony could be read by the judges of a higher court. The defense intended to appeal the case, to bring it before the Supreme Court of Tennessee, and they wanted the judges of the supreme court to be able to consider the opinions of the scientific and religious experts—that the teaching of evolution did not necessarily contradict the Bible and that the Bible should not be used for teaching science.

But then, when Clarence Darrow asked for the remainder of the day to gather the testimony and put it together, Judge Raulston indicated that he felt this was more time than was necessary. It looked as if he were going to deny the request, which meant the testimony wouldn't get into the record.

All along it had seemed to the defense lawyers as if Judge Raulston, an obvious Fundamentalist, who carried a Bible into the courtroom each day, had been siding with the prosecution. He had denied the request not to start each day with a prayer, the request to quash the indictment, and the request to bring in expert witnesses—and now this. Clarence Darrow lost his temper and barked out that he did not understand why every request the defense made "should be immediately overruled."

"I hope you do not mean to reflect upon the Court," said Raulston icily, meaning that he hoped Darrow was not implying that the judge was being unfair.

Darrow replied with a deliberate insult. "Well, Your Honor has the right to hope," he said in a sarcastic drawl.

"I have the right to do something else, perhaps," murmured Raulston, his face red with anger. Shortly afterward, he halted the trial until the following Monday. This would give the defense time to put a record of the testimony together, as they wanted to do.

Over the weekend both Bryan and Darrow issued statements to the press. Bryan stated that, "The Tennessee case has uncovered the conspiracy against the Bible Christianity—the presence of Mr. Darrow here, an avowed agnostic, both as to God and as to immortality—represents the most militant anti-Christian sentiment in the country." He charged that Darrow had "lost no opportunity to slur the intelligence of those who believe in orthodox Christianity and to hurl the charge of bigotry against everyone who objects to the teaching of evolution in the schools." He also proclaimed that "the Christian world is not going to give up its belief in God or its belief in the Bible" at the demand of men like Darrow.

Darrow replied, "Among the most prominent evolutionists of the world are multitudes of men in high standing in all the Christian churches. All of these are pronounced heretics by Mr. Bryan." Darrow insisted that, "I have no desire to have the Christian world give up its belief in God or its Bible, but at least a very large portion of the Christian world do not regard the Bible as a book of science. We know that a great majority of the intelligent Christians do not accept the literal interpretation for the whole Bible. We have learned here that a large part of the Fundamentalists do not accept it." He stated that in contrast to Bryan's charges, the defense's main interest was "that in other states, those who wish to pursue truth shall be left free to think and investigate and teach and learn."

Most of the newspaper reporters felt that the trial was all but over; packing away their notepads and typewriters, they began to leave, as did many of the visitors who had come to watch the trial. On Saturday, the radio engineers took down all of their broadcasting equipment at the courthouse. However, rumors were circulating that on Monday Judge Raulston would charge Clarence Darrow with contempt of court (disrespect for the rules of the court) for the insult he had delivered on Friday afternoon. This was a serious matter, for it could result in a fine and a jail sentence for Darrow, and it would be big news. A number of reporters stayed on to see if this would happen, and as a result, they were on hand for one of the most famous episodes in American trial history.

7

THE CLASH
OF THE TITANS:
DARROW VERSUS
BRYAN

Monday's day of trial began as many people had anticipated, with Judge Raulston charging Darrow with contempt and ordering him to post a $5,000 bond and appear in court the next day to defend himself against the charge. The lawyers of each side then wrangled for a time over the matter of the written testimony of the defense witnesses. At 11:40, Judge Raulston recessed the trial for luncheon; when it was resumed at 1:30, he announced that he had been informed that because of the large crowd there was some danger that the floor of the old courthouse building could crack and cave in, so the remainder of the trial would be held out on the courthouse lawn. The crowd surged outside.

The afternoon session began with Darrow standing up to make a public apology for the remark that had led to his being charged with contempt of court. Raulston answered with a flowery speech, accepting the apology and dropping the charge of contempt against Darrow.

Next, there was some wrangling over a large sign, clearly visible from where the jury was to sit, that said Read Your Bible. The defense wanted it removed unless, as

Darrow suggested, a sign saying Read Your Evolution could be placed next to it. The sign was finally removed.

And then the defense hurled the thunderbolt that Darrow and the others had worked out over the weekend. Arthur Garfield Hays stood up and announced, "The defense desires to call Mr. Bryan as a witness."

It was absolutely unheard of for lawyers of one side to call an attorney from the other side as a witness, and there were gasps of astonishment throughout the crowd, while Judge Raulston stared in wide-eyed surprise and William Jennings Bryan seemed to freeze in shock. The other prosecution attorneys shot to their feet, shouting objections.

The whole purpose of this move by the defense attorneys was to put evidence into the trial record, for the supreme court judges to see, that would show how difficult it could be for a teacher to make classroom instruction agree with the Bible, as teachers would have to do under the anti-evolution law. Darrow knew that even Bryan's closest friends and admirers recognized that he was far from being a deep thinker, and Darrow felt sure that in questioning Bryan he could trap him into revealing the impossibility of taking everything in the Bible as absolute truth.

When Bryan learned that the defense wanted him to testify as an expert on the Bible, he cheerfully agreed, despite the attempts of some of the other prosecution attorneys to stop him. He later stated that he had agreed so that Darrow wouldn't be able to accuse him of being fearful of facing questions about the Bible. He also planned to demand that Darrow go on the witness stand afterward so that Bryan could question *him* about his agnosticism.

Darrow began by getting Bryan to acknowledge that

he could indeed be regarded as an expert on the Bible. "I have studied the Bible for fifty years," he remarked.

"Do you claim that everything in the Bible should be literally interpreted [accepted as absolute fact]?" asked Darrow.

"I believe everything in the Bible should be accepted as given there," Bryan stated.

Darrow questioned him as to whether he really believed that a big fish or whale could swallow a man and then spit him up three days later alive and unharmed, as in the story of Jonah. Bryan acknowledged that he did believe that. Darrow asked Bryan if he believed that Joshua made the sun stand still, as the Bible states. Bryan answered that he did. Darrow then got Bryan to admit that he fully realized that the earth goes around the sun and that to stop the apparent movement of the sun it would actually have to be the earth that was stopped; but nevertheless, Bryan continued to state his belief in what the Bible said about the sun being stopped.

He was beginning to fall into Darrow's trap. When Darrow asked him if he knew how the date of the biblical flood had been worked out, Bryan replied that he'd never given it any thought, never made any calculations of his own.

"What do you think?" persisted Darrow.

"I do not think about things I don't think about," said Bryan crossly.

"Do you think about things you *do* think about?" jibed Darrow, and apparently without realizing how foolish it sounded, Bryan replied, "Well, sometimes." The audience on the courthouse lawn burst into laughter, and Bryan turned to glare at them. He was not used to being laughed at and obviously did not like it.

After a time, Attorney General Stewart stood up and

asked Judge Raulston to stop the examination. Raulston replied that to stop it would be unfair to Mr. Bryan. Darrow continued his questioning.

"How long ago was the flood, Mr. Bryan?"

Eventually, after both men had made some computations, Bryan said, "Two thousand three hundred and forty-eight years B.C." That would have been 4,273 years before 1925.

"You believe that all living things that were not contained in the ark were destroyed?"

"I think the fish may have lived," said Bryan jokingly.

Darrow stared at him. "Don't you know there are any number of civilizations that are traced back to more than five thousand years?" he asked. He was referring to ancient Egypt, China, and Mesopotamia, which had all left clear histories that had been deciphered, showing that they had existed before, during, and after the supposed flood that Bryan was insisting had wiped them out.

"I am not satisfied by any evidence that I have seen," Bryan stated. But Darrow then asked several questions that revealed Bryan had never actually bothered to study anything about the ancient races of humankind and knew nothing of prehistory.

"Don't you know that the ancient civilizations of China are six thousand or seven thousand years old at the very least?" asked Darrow. Bryan virtually shrugged this off.

"You have never in all your life made any attempt to find out about other peoples of the earth—how old their civilizations are, how long they existed on the earth, have you?" Darrow demanded.

"No, sir," said Bryan, complacently.

"You don't care how old the earth is, how old man is, and how long the animals have been here?" questioned Darrow.

"I am not much interested in that," stated Bryan.

Under Darrow's remorseless questioning, it became obvious that Bryan was almost completely ignorant of all of the proven, established facts of archeology, geology, and the origins of languages and that he did not even quite understand what gravity was. But several times he stated that he was simply uninterested in knowing about such things and was perfectly willing to accept anything in the Bible despite any evidence there might be against it.

Darrow continued to bore away at him, to establish the shallowness of his position. "Do you think the earth was made in six days?" he asked.

Surprisingly, Bryan replied, "Not six days of twenty-four hours."

Darrow looked at him in astonishment. "Doesn't it [the Bible] say so?"

"No sir," said Bryan.

From among many of the Fundamentalists in the audience there were gasps of dismay. The Book of Genesis clearly states that the Deity created everything over a period of six days, resting on the seventh, and every Fundamentalist believed—*knew*—that this meant precisely what it said: six twenty-four-hour days. But Bryan had just denied this!

Possibly fearing that Darrow now had Bryan in serious trouble, Attorney General Stewart leaped to his feet. "What is the purpose of this examination?" he demanded.

Bryan too may have felt he had made a bad mistake. Before Darrow could answer Stewart's question, Bryan himself answered it. "The purpose is to cast ridicule on everybody who believes in the Bible," he charged. "The world shall know that these gentlemen have no other purpose than ridiculing every Christian who believes in the Bible!"

"We have the purpose of preventing bigots [intolerant

persons] and ignoramuses [ignorant persons] from control-ling the education of the United States," snarled Darrow.

There was a period of sharp exchanges among the lawyers of both sides, and then Darrow was allowed to continue his questioning. Again, he asked questions in-tended to reveal how a rigid belief in some parts of the Bible could result in absurd problems. He brought up the question of Cain's wife. The Bible records how Adam was created and then Eve, that they had two sons, Cain and Abel, and that Cain murdered Abel. At that point, then, there were presumably only three people on the world; Adam, Eve, and Cain. But the Bible states that Cain went into a nearby land and found a wife. Darrow asked Bryan if he knew where this woman had come from. "Were there other people on the earth at that time?" he demanded.

"I cannot say," Bryan replied.

"There were no others recorded, but Cain got a wife," said Darrow in a sarcastic tone.

"That is what the Bible says," acknowledged Bryan.

Darrow pursued him, bringing up another puzzling contradiction in the biblical creation story: the fact that the Bible tells of "mornings and evenings" occurring *before* the sun was even created. Bryan finally snapped out: "I believe in Creation as there told, and if I am not able to explain it, I will accept it." By now, Darrow had accom-plished his purpose of showing that Bryan, presumably like most Fundamentalists, was unwilling to consider any other possibility but what was stated in the Bible, no matter how much the biblical statements might be contra-dicted by hard evidence or just common sense. To many people in the audience, Bryan had begun to appear rather foolish.

Darrow knew he had Bryan on the ropes, and he moved in for the knockout. He returned to the subject of the "days" of creation, which Bryan had admitted he did not think were actual twenty-four-hour days. "Do you think those were *literal* [actual] days?" he asked.

"My impression is they were periods," stated Bryan.

Darrow asked several more questions, then said, "Now, if you call those 'periods,' they might have been a very long time?"

"They might have been."

"The Creation might have been going on for a very long time?" urged Darrow.

"It might have continued for millions of years," Bryan acknowledged. There was another gasp from the crowd. By admitting that the "days" referred to in Genesis might have actually been periods of millions of years—which was exactly what many proevolutionists believed—Bryan had revealed that he, the champion of the unshakable truth of every word in the Bible, did not actually believe one of the Bible's clearest statements. The Fundamentalists present stared at him in dismay and confusion.

Darrow wasn't through. He went on, needling Bryan about his other beliefs. He read a passage from the Bible that tells of how God stated that as punishment for tempting Eve He would make every snake crawl on its belly from then on. "Have you any idea of how the snake went *before* that time?" Darrow asked of Bryan (it is obvious from the way a snake is constructed that it could never have done anything else *but* "crawl on its belly").

"No, sir," said Bryan.

"Do you know whether he walked on his tail or not?" Darrow asked sarcastically.

"No, sir, I have no way to know," Bryan replied, as if Darrow's question had been serious. There was an eruption of laughter from the crowd, even from many Fundamentalists, and Bryan scowled.

Darrow asked more questions, and finally, apparently unable to take any more of his adversary's goading, William Jennings Bryan shot to his feet and, shaking his fists over his head, angrily shrieked out that Darrow's only purpose in all this was "to slur the Bible!"

"I object to your statement!" roared Darrow. "I am examining you on your fool ideas that no intelligent Christian on earth believes!"

Nearly everyone present rose in a storm of shouting and arm waving, each faction voicing its opinion. Bryan and Darrow were shaking their fists at each other. Apparently fearing that a riot might begin, Judge Raulston banged his gavel and bellowed, "Court is adjourned until nine o'clock tomorrow morning!"

Bryan had come off very badly. Newspaper accounts of his responses to Darrow's questions made him look like a simpleton. According to most of the reporters present, he had been completely demolished by Darrow's questioning. One of the reporters, who was an admirer of Bryan, wrote that Bryan was "a crushed and broken man." Another said he had been "humbled and humiliated." And he had clearly disappointed many of his Fundamentalist followers. Most of them carefully kept away from him as he left the courthouse area. The few who did approach him did so only to scold him for having denied the biblical truth of the "days" of creation.

8

THE RESULT
OF THE TRIAL AND ITS
EFFECT ON THE NATION
IN MODERN TIMES

Bryan had not been officially dismissed as a witness, so he was to go back on the stand the following day; afterward he intended to call Darrow to the stand, subject *him* to questioning, and then make a final, rousing speech to close the prosecution's case. But none of these things happened. Several of the Dayton town officials secretly met with Judge Raulston and urged him to somehow end the trial at once. Feeling was running high in the town, death threats had been made against both Darrow and Bryan, and the officials feared what might happen. So when the trial continued, Raulston announced he had decided that the examination of Bryan by Darrow had really shed no light on the actual issue of the trial—whether or not Scopes had broken the law—so no further examination would be permitted by either side, and all of the words spoken by Darrow and Bryan the previous day would be removed from the official record of the trial. This meant there was nothing left to do except for the jury to bring in a verdict. The trial was about to end.

Many people would have been surprised to know that Darrow and the other defense attorneys were actually somewhat fearful that the jury might find Scopes not guilty. They didn't want this to happen because they wanted to be able to have the trial continued before the Tennessee Supreme Court. The American Civil Liberties Union's whole purpose in having the trial was to have the anti-evolution law struck down, of course. If Scopes were found not guilty, the law would still be in force, and the whole trial would really have been pointless. So Clarence Darrow made a short speech to the jury, pointing out that there really was no doubt that John Scopes had broken the law; he should be found guilty so that the case could be appealed and a decision on the anti-evolution law made by the high court. The jury complied, Judge Raulston sentenced Scopes to pay a fine of $100, and asked him if he had anything to say.

"Your Honor," said Scopes, "I feel that I have been convicted of violating an unjust statute [law]. I will continue in the future as I have in the past, to oppose this law in any way I can. Any other action would be in violation of my ideal of academic freedom—that is, to teach the truth as guaranteed in our constitution, of personal and religious freedom. I think the fine is unjust."

Defense attorney Arthur Hays officially requested the court's permission to appeal the case to the Tennessee Supreme Court, and the judge granted permission. Several of the lawyers and others present then made short statements.

The statement made by William Jennings Bryan showed a sense of fairness and a strong belief in democracy. "Here has been fought out a little case of little consequence as a case," he said, "but the world is interested because it raises an issue, and that issue will someday be settled right, whether it is settled on our side or the other side. It is going to be settled right." He predicted that "the people will determine this issue." He finished by saying he felt that "no matter what our views may be, we ought not only desire, but pray, that that which is right will prevail, whether it be our way or somebody else's." He was soundly applauded.

Clarence Darrow, in his statement, remarked that "there is much that Mr. Bryan has said that is true." But he went on to say, "I think this case will be remembered because it is the first case of this sort since we stopped trying people in America for witchcraft, because here we have done our best to turn back the tide that has sought to force itself upon this modern world, of testing every fact in science by a religious dictum [opinion]."

Shortly thereafter, the judge's gavel banged for the final time. On Tuesday, July 21, 1925, the "great Monkey Trial" came to an end.

It was generally regarded at that time as the most famous court trial in world history. More than two hundred news reporters and other writers had attended it, and more words were sent across the Atlantic and Pacific oceans about it, via cable, than had ever been sent for anything else that had happened in the United States. A great number of prominent people and organizations had commented on it, chiefly on the side of evolution. World-famous scientists such as Albert Einstein made statements deploring the passage of the law.

Five days after the trial ended, William Jennings Bryan died in his sleep. Many people felt he had "died of a broken heart" because of the humiliation Clarence Darrow had put upon him, which is highly doubtful, of course. Bryan suffered from the disease known as *diabetes mellitus*, which can cause fatal strokes and heart failure.

Just about a year later, the appeal on the Scopes case, conducted by Darrow and the other defense lawyers, was made to the Tennessee Supreme Court. Four judges considered the records of the Scopes Trial and the arguments of the lawyers and made their decisions. Two ruled that the

anti-evolution law was not contradictory to the constitution and that Scopes had broken it. One ruled that it was
not contradictory to the constitution but gave the opinion
that Scopes had not broken it because the concept of
evolution did not actually deny Divine Creation and
therefore did not break the law as it was stated. The fourth
judge ruled that the law was unconstitutional. Thus, inasmuch as a three-judge majority had agreed with the constitutionality of the law, it remained part of the law of
Tennessee. But as far as the "punishment" of John Scopes
was concerned, the supreme court overturned Judge Raulston's ruling on a technicality, and the fine against Scopes
was revoked. (Scopes never returned to his job as a high
school teacher, however. With the help of a number of
scientists, he was able to attend the University of Chicago;
he became a geologist.)

The defense attorneys had planned, if they lost their
appeal to the Supreme Court of Tennessee, to carry the
case on up to the highest court in the land, the United
States Supreme Court. But to their dismay, the Tennessee
Supreme Court used a technicality to make this impossible. And so the "Monkey Trial" hadn't accomplished what
the people who had started it had hoped it would do. The
anti-evolution law was still in force in Tennessee, and
throughout the nation many school officials began to be
very careful about the teaching of evolution lest they have
trouble from Fundamentalists.

Leading Fundamentalists mounted a new attack to put
anti-evolution laws into every state and eventually to have a
national anti-evolution law passed by Congress. They were
successful in having a law passed in Mississippi in 1926,
but bills for similar laws introduced into the legislatures of
Kentucky and Louisiana that year were voted down. Over
the next few years two other states passed anti-evolution
laws, but then the impetus of the Fundamentalist push

died away. By the 1930s the whole Fundamentalist–evolutionist conflict had been pushed into the background, and in the 1940s and 1950s, many people didn't even realize there had ever been such a conflict. Any reference to the Scopes Trial made to someone born after 1925 would generally have been meaningless.

But in the long run, the Scopes Trial had been a victory for the Fundamentalists. Although they succeeded in getting anti-evolution laws into only four states, they had managed to practically halt the teaching of evolution in most public schools throughout the country. Most textbook publishers, fearful of running afoul of Fundamentalist-dominated schoolboards and losing sales, took almost all mention of Darwin and evolution out of their textbooks for the next thirty-five years; and most teachers, especially in high schools, fearful of being fired if they taught evolution (as some were), covered it only very briefly and in many cases not at all. It was only those people who went into science as a profession or those who made a point of looking deeply into the subject who became aware of the enormous amount of evidence, continuously growing, to prove the fact of evolution, the age of the earth, and other matters that the Fundamentalists contested.

Then, in 1957, there was an event that changed everything. The Soviet Union launched Sputnik, the first artificial satellite, showing that their space program was far ahead of that of the United States, and Americans were made painfully aware that they were lagging in science and technology. There was a sudden crash program to catch up, and responsibility for upgrading scientific education in the United States was placed in the hands of scientific groups. One of the results of this was that the biology textbooks of the 1960s suddenly became chock-full of information on evolution and the work of Charles Darwin and others, and evolution was once again being taught as an established scientific fact in most schools throughout the nation. By the late 1960s, the anti-evolution laws had been quietly repealed in the states where they had been in force.

Thus, the situation was almost exactly as it had been in the 1920s, and exactly the same thing happened. Fundamentalists had been relatively quiet during the 1940s and 1950s because they did not feel particularly threatened, but suddenly they were once again confronted with the presence of a subject that they felt menaced the religious beliefs and morality of their children and was a danger to the well-being of the entire country. It is estimated that in the late 1960s there were at least 50 million Fundamentalists in the United States, many of them probably the children and grandchildren of Fundamentalists of the Scopes Trial period, and during the following decade they put together another effort to attack and rout the teaching of evolution.

But the Fundamentalists of the 1970s and 1980s took a different approach from those of the 1920s. At the time of the Scopes trial, the nation's newspapers and magazines had generally portrayed Fundamentalists as ignorant bigots who were simply against science, and the modern-day Fundamentalists wanted to avoid having such a thing happen to them. So this time they tried to show that they were actually on the side of science. Insisting that evolution was merely a theory, they charged that other theories deserved to have equal time with it, and they offered what they called the theory of "scientific creationism." This had been developed by several Fundamentalists who, while not actually scientists, had done a great deal of study of various fields of science. Scientific creationism is essentially an attempt to show that most scientific evidence supports the biblical story of Divine Creation better than it supports evolution. There were attempts made in several states to get scientific creationism taught in schools along with the teaching of evolution, and bills insisting that this should be done were introduced into the legislatures of a number of states. Laws requiring the teaching of scientific creationism were passed in Louisiana and Arkansas in the early 1980s.

Many Americans felt that it was only fair to teach two contrasting viewpoints this way. But many scientists and educators were quick to point out that if "fairness" were all that mattered, it would be only fair to teach in schools that the earth is flat because there are some people who still believe that. This isn't done because, as everyone knows, the earth isn't flat, and no one wants to teach something that is wrong to high school and college students. And the overwhelming majority of scientists and educators throughout the United States insisted that scientific creationism was also wrong—that it was nothing more than thinly disguised religion with no scientific evidence at all to back it up.

A number of people in Arkansas—scientists, teachers, businessmen, and ministers—wanted to test the new law that forced the teaching of scientific creationism in their state, in hope of having it overturned. And so, in 1981, there was a court trial. The Scopes Trial, which had been largely forgotten after fifty-six years, was now recalled by many reporters and columnists, and the new trial was quickly labeled "the Scopes II Trial." Once again, the American Civil Liberties Union furnished the lawyers to do battle for science against religious opinion. There was no one like either Bryan or Darrow this time, but now scientists and ministers were allowed to testify in favor of evolution and against scientific creationism. And on January 5, 1982, the judge hearing the case (there was no jury involved) ruled that scientific creationism was actually religion, not science, and therefore could not be taught in Arkansas' public schools inasmuch as that would violate the state constitution. The law was thus abolished.

The law that had been passed in Louisiana was taken before the United States Supreme Court, and on June 19, 1987, the court ruled, as the judge in Arkansas had, that scientific creationism was not truly a scientific theory but actually a religious viewpoint and could not be taught in any U.S. public schools, as that would violate the separation of religion from government that is ordered by the United States Constitution.

So the Fundamentalists were defeated, and their effort to pass more laws was blocked. However, the conflict is far from over. Fundamentalists still insist that there is really no such thing as evolution and that scientific creationism provides a better answer than any theory of evolution. On the other hand, scientists throughout the world regard the evidence for evolution as overwhelming and absolutely undoubtable.

There is every possibility that, in the future, Fundamentalists will once again wage an effort to make their beliefs prevail over the teaching of evolution, and scientists and others will rush to stand against them. And the memory of the 1925 Scopes Trial will again be recalled.

PHOTOGRAPHY CREDITS
A NOTE ABOUT SOURCES
BIBLIOGRAPHY
INDEX

PHOTOGRAPHY CREDITS

Photographs courtesy of: Wide World Photo: pp. 1 top, 4, 8, 16; The Bettmann Archive: pp. 1 bottom, 9 bottom, 14; New York Public Library, Picture Collection: pp. 2 top, 11 bottom; American Civil Liberties Union: p. 2 bottom; Bryan College, Clark H. Robinson Collection: pp. 3, 15; UPI/Bettmann Newsphotos: pp. 5, 6, 7, 9 top, 10, 11 top, 12, 13.

A NOTE
ABOUT SOURCES

Quotes from the attorneys' speeches and arguments during the trial of *Tennessee v. John Thomas Scopes* are taken from Oren Metzger and William Hilleary's book *The World's Most Famous Court Trial* (1925), reprinted in 1978 by the Rhea County (Tennessee) Historical Society.

BIBLIOGRAPHY

Allen, Leslie H. *Bryan and Darrow at Dayton: The Records and Documents of the Bible-Evolution Trial.* 1925. Reprint. Russell and Russell, 1967.

Armitage, Angus. *The World of Copernicus.* New York: Mentor, 1959. (Lecturer in the Department of History and Philosophy of Science, University College, London.)

Cherny, Robert W. *A Righteous Cause: The Life of William Jennings Bryan.* Boston: Little, Brown, 1985. (Professor of history, San Francisco State University.)

Clark, Ronald W. *The Survival of Charles Darwin: A Biography of a Man and an Idea.* New York: Random House, 1984. (Biographer of Einstein, Freud, and others.)

de Camp, L. Sprague. *The Great Monkey Trial.* Garden City, NY: Doubleday, 1968. (Author of *Science in America, Ancient Ruins and Archaeology, The Ancient Engineers, Energy and Power, Engines.*)

Gould, Stephen Jay. "Evolution as Fact and Theory." Chap. 5, section 19 of *Hens' Teeth and Horses' Toes: Further Reflections in Natural History.* New York: W.W. Norton and Co., 1983.

Gould, Stephen Jay. "Moon, Mann, and Otto." Chap. 5, section 21 of *Hens' Teeth and Horses' Toes: Further Reflections in Natural History.* New York: W.W. Norton and Co., 1983. (Professor of geology, biology, and history of science, Harvard University.)

Kurland, Gerald. *Clarence Darrow: Attorney for the Damned.* Charlotteville, NY: SamHar Press, 1972.

Metzger, Oren and William Hilleary. *The World's Most Famous Court Trial: Tennessee Evolution Case.* 1925. Reprint. Rhea County (Tennessee) Historical Society, 1978. (A word-for-word report of attorneys' speeches and arguments, testimony of witnesses, etc., compiled from newspaper records.)

Ruse, Michael, ed. *But Is It Science? The Philosophical Question in the Creation/Evolution Controversy.* Buffalo, NY: Prometheus Press, 1988. (Professor of history and philosophy, University of Guelph [Canada]; fellow, American Association for the Advancement of Science; fellow, Royal Society of Canada.)

Sagarin, Edward, and Brandt Aymar. "John Scopes." Chap. 21 in *A Pictorial History of the World's Great Trials.* New York: Bonanza, 1967. (Professor of sociology at City College of New York; Brandt Aymar, editor.)

Stone, Irving. *Clarence Darrow for the Defense.* Garden City, NY: Doubleday, 1941. (Regarded as the definitive biography of Darrow.)

INDEX